Robert Dickinson

Micrographia

First published in 2010
by Waterloo Press (Hove)
9E Wick Hall
Furze Hill
Hove BN3 1NG

Printed in Palatino 11pt by
One Digital
54 Hollingdean Road
East Sussex BN2 4AA

Cover design © Waterloo Design 2010
Cover illustration: detail from a mural on the Berlin Wall
Photograph © 2010

Robert Dickinson is hereby identified as author of this
work in accordance with Section 77 of the Copyright,
Designs and Patents Act 1988

A CIP record for this book is available
from the British Library

ISBN 978-1-906742-12-6

Acknowledgements

Acknowledgements are due to the editors of the following publications where some of these poems first appeared: *The Rialto, Smiths Knoll, The Independent on Sunday, The Lung, Poetry South.*

Thanks are due to Simon Jenner at Waterloo Press for commissioning this book. I'd also like to thank Brendan Cleary, Bernadette Cremin, John Davies, Andrew Dilger, Naomi Foyle, Robert Hamberger, Lee Harwood, David Hellens, Maria Jastrzebska, John McCulloch, Alan Morrison, John O'Donoghue, Catherine Smith, Tom Sutcliffe, Janet Sutherland, Joby Talbot, and Jackie Wills, among others.

By the same author

Poetry

Szyzgy with Andrew Dilger (Notus, 2001)

Libretti

Path of Miracles, Joby Talbot (Chester Music, 2005)

Fiction

The Noise of Strangers (Myriad Editions, 2010)

Contents

Micrographia

Aetiology

Where does it hurt? In Battersea
for a start, a hot tingle
like the afterglow of a slap.
Scar tissue in Wimbledon sidestreets,
small palpitations in coastal towns
with roads ending in sand.

And then the raw wound of Streatham,
healed and annealed.
Croydon, Surrey and Mitcham, Surrey:
patchwork recoveries that ache
in an East wind, if it rains.
There are more: something like a bruise
that stretched for three days
along Carshalton High Street,
a constriction of the muscles
next to Victoria Station.
But only one gives me trouble:
Woodbourne Avenue, between Garrard's Road
and the post office. Yes, there.

Still life with racing pages

Boxes in the hallway, horses on TV.
His chosen donkeys stumble to the line
too late to matter. "Fix". Everything's fixed,
except his leg, and the colour contrast
turning psychedelic as the sound dies.
The set's been dud for years, and so has he.
"How are *you*?" Hitting the basket's rim
with another crumpled slip. "Working?
Happy?" Work's a con, happy is stupid,
and all the shops are daylight robbery.
He had a job once, printing. Never again.
Ink poisons your blood. "They don't tell you that.
Need a new camera?" He'll know someone,
their face if not their name. "A hi-fi, cheap?
I bought this last week. D'you know what it is?"
Four sugars in his tea. I measure them out,
focussing on the screen as he adjusts
the spare false teeth he found outside a pub.

Green horses idle on a scarlet track.

Love and hate, 1977

That was the year he tattooed his hands
and slept on his Nan's sofa,
nervous as the guinea pigs he'd once fed at school.

That was the summer he shaved his head
and didn't get a job,
frowning over the paperbacks
he stole from the junkshop and didn't finish.

The Exhibitionist, The Naked Lunch,
The Tight White Collar, Dr. No...

His Nan said: "Rough diamond, Good lad really"
and laughed when he hid on the fire escape
as her friends called for bingo.

That was the year he carried a knife
into a car park,
jabbed once and ran, without looking back.

That was the year of waiting and television,
of not touching a drop;
a long time ago he'll tell you.

He twists his hands as he talks, hiding the words.

Blind forty

The days aren't long enough
or too long.
Tonight she'll half cook
something frozen.
But I'm clean, she says
as the rooms fill with dust.

It's just a phase:
ten years under
the relentless weather,
lost in the supermarket's ranked exotica,
the dust thickening.

A squat white dog,
bullet headed,
tranquilised,
nuzzles the chair it loves
and will one day eat.

Without intent

I was there for the view. All that empty space
sweeping down to the glare of the Hyundai showroom
and the all-night shop where they know what I buy;
the black grass, the dim light by the swings,
the trees at my back like a wall
with nothing behind it. And the noise the wind makes
when it drops, like a thief in a downstairs room,
scared and trying not to breathe. I like it,
the way the path winds here, so far from the street
the traffic's a whisper, a warning
that anything might happen. The city's still there,
but distant, and people would swear under oath
you never left home or they watched you all night
sitting just left of the dartboard. The usual two pints.
I was there for the view, and the quiet. Just standing:
ten minutes solitary, then back to the natter,
that's all. And the knife's for an apple
I'll cut into quarters, sooner or later.

Precautions

Let the phone ring twice before you hang up;
give the prearranged knock at the time I'll advise
in a letter to be left in the park
under the raised left heel of the late mayor's statue.
Don't come straight here. Come via the alley
where that grey cat sits on the fence in all weathers
and will not be stroked, turn left at the lockups
with the Maoist graffiti and dark green Fiesta
turning to rust on its bricks. Doubleback,
as if you've changed your mind, then come anyway.
Further instructions have been left with the newsagents
where you once bought the milk, a sky blue envelope
addressed to "Sandra". Remember that name.
You might notice a difference when I open the door.
Show no surprise. Burn this. Burn everything.

Your grief

Tell it to the man in the driver's seat
of the white Astra parked by the off-licence
as he turns the pages of yesterday's Star
without looking away from the door of those flats.

Tell it to the seven o'clock wind
gusting over the emerald lips
of four bottles of imported lager
left half-finished in a jeweller's doorway.

Tell it to your reflection
in the sheet glass of bakers' and stationers',
to your hunched shoulders, to your head
bowed as if it was raining.

See its likeness in the high street
among the blankets and uncollected rubbish,
bargains nobody wanted, nobody wants —

or scar your hands. Get something pierced.

Evasions of the nightingale

A white plastic gutter
filled with sludge;

a bass drone
from the motorway

and summer coming on
like influenza.

The great forests dwindle,
the copses, the walled gardens.

These are thin times:
the streetwise, nervy foxes

digging for meat from plastic sacks
are not more careful.

We stay off the ground,
we give nothing away,

we coo like pigeons
on the flat garage roofs.

The pale amateur cellist
with a local reputation

waits on her patio
bow at hand, microphone set.

Just in time
I remember not to sing.

Biopic

1

It starts with a flashback of one small room,
a view of the window from knee height,
a woman I've never seen
reaching down in soft focus.
Outside, Becton gasworks
stands in for somewhere east of Prague.

Memories. Details. This and that.
Soldiers tramping to garrisons,
market day peasants, drunk and ready to fight,
schoolteachers hoarding busts of Goethe,
speaking their mother tongue with a foreign accent,
their servants' babies
left for dead on the orphanage doorstep...
I remember it all
as if I read it yesterday.

Under the clogged feet of extras
the burnt rubber of yesterday's car chase
visible, if you know where to look.

2

They skip the uneventful rest,
the twelve year stretch
to the end of adolescence.
Days fall from the calendar,
miserly confetti.
Remember, I had to live them.

Nineteen hundred and five, for instance:
I read Ibsen and Bergson and young Thomas Mann,
played viola in a schoolfriend's quartet,

studied Latin and Spanish, went four times
to a brothel in the workers' quarter,
wrote papers they ignored in Berlin
and half a sonata for piano and cello,
fell in love with the cellist's sister, almost turned Catholic,
proposed unsuccessfully to my landlady's daughter,
worked for the Civil Service like everybody else,
was disinherited on two separate occasions,
forgiven each time by sentimental parents.

They'll show me drinking beer, and singing.

3

Hackney will pass for Vienna.
From significant talk with a friend,
a composite of everyone I knew,
I look up from my famous desk,
the famous realisation about to dawn
in the sweep of a tight close up.
"If you are right, everything will change..."

The truth is beer and singing.
I woke up sick,
considered the intestinal slop and gurgle
of my stomach, its Brownian motion,
and knelt in the water closet,
the door kicked shut to the laughter of servants.
And it came to me then,
that catchphrase formula
about movement and light,
and so much for the dignity of science.

4

And now the love interest, a trade-off
with the crowds in the dark,
a courtship rewritten to fit
the conventions of a country
whose language I'll never learn.
Ten years' work in a single scene
against a kiss in real time.
A fair swap. I'll take it.

Stop the film. The girl I kiss
is wrong, is prettier
than the stolid Gertrudes, pale Angelas
whose bodies lay under mine
still, as if for surgery;
who'd learnt the sorry truth
from wives of brusque husbands;
serious men, wary of pleasure.
Stop the film. Hold this moment
until it burns.
                    The girl I kiss
opens her mouth and pushes against me
through the unfamiliar, period dress
designed to restrict precisely this movement.

5

Those small town intellectuals
minding their ps and qs
in roomfuls of approved classics,
culture with a capital K.
Remember those pioneers?

If only they'd heard of the unconscious
and its buried discontents
(the best fad since mesmerism);
if only they'd seen the gawky, grey nudes

of the newest fêted painter
(but he came from their town,
they didn't know he was born).

If only they'd grasped, as the century
stamped into its difficult teens,
how their idols would vanish
and their manners would crack,
how they would turn from imagined audiences
to find the scenery had changed
with a *trompe-l'oile* transition
out of Georges Méliès
in the jump cut of August.

6

We'll skip the war.
I kept my head down, my eyes shut.
The limbless on their carts
are not part of my story.
I dropped coins at their side
and moved on
while the coins lost value as they fell,
the clink of their metal
like the comedy note of a cinema pianist;
a value so small
the numbers were imaginary,
were guesswork, ten to the power of minus whatever.
Later there was money in sacks,
more noughts than the speed of light in inches,
ersatz coffee, bread that was not bread.
I kept my head down. I had my work.

7

A null experiment on the aether drift,
inconclusive reports from the smoke chamber...
The classical dream was dead:
there is no finite sphere
where speed and mass and energy
dance one-two-three, one-two-three
like a triumvirate of angels
on the needle's infinite point.
You'll see an equation across a board,
standing for everything
you are not expected to know.
The rest is metaphor,
therefore wrong.
                    But I say
the universe is a like a tablecloth
on shifting sand. The world
is the possibility of the world,
the chance of it happening.
I say: consider light moving through water,
the properties of rods and clocks
in the dilation of time.
They are only words.
So here is a formula concise as a slogan,
meaning nothing, and part of everything.

8

Politics as broken windows.
From bad to worse,
from bad to slightly worse.
My students marching
to that song about the Wessel pimp,
to blood and soil and the stab in the back.
Daily recalibrations of shock,
a slow thickening of clouds overhead,
until you realise, glancing up,

it is midnight in the afternoon.
I saw the black sky, ran for the West
and that's all you'll see:
a last minute dash,
forged papers for added suspense
and the end of the old world behind me
like a storm about to break.

Here are the newsreels to put me in context.
The newsreels are fake.

9

The spinning headlines
end with a bomb, the saturated white
of syndicated photographs.
I was north of that desert,
those islands where the second war stopped,
beautiful, inhuman.

So we'll jump five years
because all that happens now
is the start of the slide
into research that leads nowhere.
We'll jump five years. Make it ten.

Not much happened.
Each day waking up
to respectable exile,
living well in the house I was given
too old for a new language,
happy in work that went nowhere
among considerate strangers
Home had shifted east, changed its name,
become silence or death, banners
hung across the ruined academies.
Battersea Park stands in for New England.

10

Old age is unconvincing —
the skin too wattled, the hair too white,
the face too carefully serene.
The view of the street
(extras in costume, not enough cars)
unconvincing, shot at dawn.

I never believed it, even then.

Look closely at my hands.
However much they tremble, they are young.

The tale of the giant's head

Jack-Without-Land rolled the head of the giant
into the sack he'd brought from the village
and, sack on his shoulder, set off down the mountain.

The head was as large as a boar from the forest;
with each heavy step Jack felt at his back
lips writhing like eels, the brush of its eyelids.

Tired, he set the head on some rocks.
He stretched himself on the sloping grass
to think of the welcome they'd give in the valley.

Jack woke at sunrise, stronger, refreshed.
The head in the sack seemed no larger now
than the old hunting dog he had buried that spring.

But still it was heavy, and the village distant.
Come noon, hungry, he stopped at a stream
to moisten the crusts from the giant's table.

And when he set off the head was lighter than ever
and shrunk to the size of a prize-winning cabbage.
It bounced at his back all the way to the foothills

where Jack paused again and looked at the village,
further off, it seemed, than he remembered.
There was the fading rumble of carts in the forest,

the neighing of horses on the old forest road.
Tiny clothes and furniture, broken pots
dropped at the side of a ribbon of mud

as if all the town's children were tired of playing.
Jack waited for them to run out and greet him
but the village seemed empty and quiet and small.

Nobody came. He took the head from the bag.
It balanced on his palm, the size of an apple,
its eyes tight as a fist, its mouth a long smile.

*

He stood among houses that reached to his shoulder
as a thing like a mouse yapped and jumped at his ankle
and crows from the rooftops shouted, "Curse, curse."

Proofs

For we remember Saint Euphorion
whose body stank to high heaven
sweeter than attar of roses
in the midsummer heat by Narbonne.
That year, the harvest did not fail.

We have seen miracles
from men lower than dirt:
Clotus of Avignon,
saint of by-roads and plague pits,
who drank only the water
in which he bathed his rotted feet —
granted thereby a vision of paradise.

And Sigibert, whom our late king,
Chilperic the Cloth-Eared,
staked for a week in the courtyard,
who sang hymns to the falling snow
long after his tongue was thrown for the dogs.

Or Eparchius, the force of whose prayers
caused a gibbet to crumble like sand
in the winter of the great storms,
sparing that thief who then robbed
the Bishop of Metz, whose name I forget.
Truly, the ways of the Lord are strange.

Brief and bitter lives flare like night fires.
In the third year of the famine
I took the hard road to Autun
and saw hooded angels
tallying the roadside dead.
At times He comes so close
we touch His light as if with fingertips.
They say a man in Paris keeps the tongue.

The Taxi Driver year

Nothing eased the burden of ironing like violence:
fourteen crumpled workshirts smoothed flat,
Travis Bickle crazier by the sleeve.
The five with polycotton mix
I finished before he'd even thought of guns.
The 100% cotton, left for last,
took four scenes each, or five,
as my rhythm slowed to the pace
of that looping saxophone score.

What else could be done with all that time?
At least I didn't recite the dialogue
or stage a face-off with the bathroom mirror.
Even after the twenty-seventh Sunday,
a whole year gone, I didn't identify.
As I folded away the board
de Niro would strap a knife to his ankle;
I'd look out at the lights of Croydon
shining in the distance, a promised city.

I am a bullet

Performance. James Fox going Cockney,
all posture and montage on rented Betamax.
East End machismo, the hard man in his gaff.

We have the victim's POV. Fox is Chas
somewhere between credo and renunciation.

He is about to kill.

Chas is a face, known.
Afterwards he pulls on a bloody shirt,
dyes his hair, pretends to leave town.

And John from my office, the tosser, thrilled
when Charlie Kray walked into his local,
slum royalty holding court at a back table.
I shook hands with him.

A face, with a face's ambition:
to be something in life. Such as death.

Business objectives

This is my desk. This is my chair.
This is my telephone. *A process,*
a framework to review and praise.
This is my keyboard and mousepad.
These are my hands. *Commitment,*
mutual responsibility
quantified. What it is
that has to be done. My password.
For clarity these are divided
into examples of words:
ACHIEVE DRIVE MOTIVATE
INCREASE LEAD GENERATE.
The filing cabinets are locked.
Objectives are set for the coming period
where rotation may not occur.
These are my pencils and paperclips,
my in-tray and excuses.
A positive customer experience,
significantly enhanced penetration
of relevant areas. Ask the questions:
What will success look like?
How will I know, how can I tell or measure?
This is my name on the letterhead,
this is the stamp with my number.
Should you have any queries
a blank form is attached.

A gone concern

In the days before I was a gone concern
I wore suits so black they dimmed the room.

Work emptied the time; from my high desk,
topped with leather, photographs and pens,

I'd stretch to shift the slow ache from my back
and notice sunlight spreading like damp

across the carpet cleaners wouldn't touch.
Each Christmas I left them bottles of Scotch.

*

Migraine, insomnia and paper cuts.
Haemorrhoids, insomnia, paper cuts.

But that was the price as I inked in red
precise marginalia under the anglepoise.

*

Until that Thursday morning I overslept
for the first time in my waking life

and went out to my garden, surprised that I had one,
to bury my work ethic under a greenhouse.

*

My left arm soft with a cheesy necrosis
I blinked in a sun nobody paid for

watching the workers pack tables in vans,
the last one to leave unscrewing the light-bulb.

Backsliding

I stubbed my toe at the door
to the Centre of Excellence;
choked in its thin, recycled air.

I stood in the foyer
by the shrines to the exemplary dead,
waiting for the word from on high,

le mot juste, that bastard
of protestant ethics
and a classical education —

like having exactly the right money, always;
knowing the unlikeliest sign
for this thing, that feeling.

I waited for hours, then days,
worrying at the silences,
the nuanced whispers.

These days I live in the suburb,
preferring its indistinct greys,
the metaphorical fog of its mornings;

I carry the folding money
of approximation,
welcome in all the shops.

Kind of. Sort of. You know.

Rappaccini's son-in-law

The girl was poison. One kiss
left me dizzy for weeks, vomiting
yellow bile on the half hour
as my kidneys turned to gloop.
But I couldn't resist. After radiotherapy

I got the nod from her old man,
waited till my hair grew back
and popped the question. She laughed
in that crazy, friendless way she had
and said OK. We shook hands;

I came round in Emergency
after three months of touch-and-go
where I'd raved about transfusions
and scalding formication.
Her old man said he'd booked the church.

On the big day I could walk a few paces.
She was there in her bubble
and sterilised dress. The bridesmaids
fumbled with gas masks in the aisle,
the minister was flicking through Merck's . . .

My doctors were at the reception,
they nodded and winked, like I'd become
their private, dirty joke. I waved goodbye
and stumbled up the hotel stairs
to the room sick with flowers, where she waited.

The missed exhibitions

There were so many, for years —
Invisible Art, Grey Installations,
Myopic Painters of The Quattrocentro —
I missed them all.
Wall Photography, Inventing The Face,
Nothing Much Happening,
openings and retrospectives,
considerations, reconsiderations
in galleries that could have been
in China, on the moon.
I found time for *Gun Fury, Forced Entry,*
and *Sob Sister III* at the multiplex
but not for *De Chirico*
and the futurist tradition two streets on,
or *The Lost Sketchbooks of Angelica Kaufmann,*
Young Manchester, Entropic Destiny,
Masterworks From The Northern California
Secure Life Pension Fund Collection,
The Walthamstow Surrealists...
It's time to be serious. Any day now.

Three pieces with Spanish titles

Sol y sombra

In a narrow bed I didn't make,
shielded from the Autovia's dust
by a dazzle of buildings,
the difference between sun and shadow
is absolute, the livid heat
is part surrounding air,
part state of mind,
and I think for no reason
of a sick beast in a ring of sand,
the flash attendants
wheeling at his flanks, his death
a shadow in a suit of lights.
Each movement jars
the headboard against the pitted wall.

Aburrimiento

The sun. The sand the colour of cement. The blocks of apartments
waiting for nightfall. The sun. The wind bringing dust from the
playing field. The single handclap to the radio's flamenco. The
crane on the horizon that has not moved for days. The sun. The
quiet streets leading from blank hotels. The bars waiting for
nightfall. A cloud, the size of a hand.

Se vende

Residents pass
the boarded door
of the Quo Vadis
Karaoke Bar.
Such faded lack
of elegance —
I sang there once
(*My Way*, in French).

Corruption

The flowers, a last show of respect,
die at our feet as we exchange
our guesses at his unpaid debts.

At least we keep our faces straight
despite the body's rising stink,
that rotten corpse we laid in state.

What if we never said a thing
of how we hated him alive,
or dead, how we still hated him?

Our English understated style
kept us laughing at his jokes
and hid the sneer behind the smile.

We took our wages, cast our votes,
if there's a crime, it isn't us,
it's all that bastard in the box.

And if the money wasn't his
it pays for us to be here now,
holding back authentic tears

for money that will not be ours.

Eschatology

Him there, with the Hapsburg chin
and Iron Maiden T-shirt, yes, him,
punching in answers at the quiz machine:

he isn't pushing those buttons at random,
despite the fact he loses every time.
There's method to his concentration.

And it's not a case of what he thinks he knows:
he's searching for the pattern,
the underlying sequence of the world.

Who played what part or won the match
is not the point.
The point is whether A should follow B

or B should be repeated seven times,
then C, then A, then C again,
and so on in a perfect combination

that, discovered, will fold the universe
into a single, fading point of light,
saving him from ever going home.

Fraud

When the boat overturns,
as on some nights it does,
she always goes under.

And what wakes up is either
not her but a likeness,
a word-perfect impostor,

or her as a ghost
in familiar rooms
that should have been emptied

but are somehow unchanged.
Why do they think they can see her?
Why do they still use her name?

Norfolk conspiracy

They filmed the first moon landing in my field
and over there, they buried Kennedy,
the *real* Kennedy, back in '62.
I was a kid then, hiding in ditches
as black cars cruised by hedgerows and canals
or parked six deep across the village green,
looking, it was said, for good locations,
for people who would never be believed.
They found us. There were boxes in storage
labelled "Hoffa", "McCartney", and "Monroe" —
I played beside them in Geoff Miller's barn
the summer Jack Oswald's boy went missing —
he came back rich and drank himself to death.
Happier times. Not much has happened since:
crops come and go, and winter clears the fields,
the houses shrink beneath the heavy skies
and, one by one, the old folk disappear.

The painter, Sebastian Kohler

The paint will not keep still. The figures move
however thickly he smears it on.
Overnight they shift, their expressions change.

He weights them with cloaks and mantels,
winter overcoats, a suitcase in each hand,
ridiculous towering hats. Still they move.

They won't keep still, are pensive
when they're meant to laugh,
laughing when he wants them serious.

He puts them in mazes, courtyards without doors,
gardens fringed with bramble,
forests where he knows there are wolves.

He doesn't paint the wolves. He hears them
snuffling beyond the canvas, trying to catch
his scent of oils and bitter sweat, the smoke of burning paper.

He works until the paint is inches deep,
and when he wakes, his people have moved again,
edged along the abstracts of his walls

another step towards his grey horizon,
the heavy clouds, his thin and grasping trees.

The fall of Troy

Forget what you've heard:
Helen, the ten-year siege, the trick with the horse,
none of that happened.
The truth is, Troy fell in a week,
the king fled south.
His court stayed on to kneel before the Greeks.

Give us Helen, and we'll leave.
But there was no Helen,
and they'd forgotten how to leave.
Out on the beach their ships decayed
while they ransacked our kitchens,
looking for a reason to be there,

blunting their axe heads
on linen chests and cellar doors;
stripping the houses bare
of gold, of brass, of iron, then of stone.
And Helen? She was never here,
and Priam died a hundred years ago...

Executions and reprisals, executions.
Our king in the South,
calling upon the astonished gods,
an old man wailing in foreign harbours.
And this went on for days, and then for years;
when there was no-one left to kill they called it peace.

0-1-0

Sponsored by the downtown tattoo shop
that put the biker mottoes on his chest,
he's crossed two states to bulk an undercard
under ring lights hotter than an August noon.

The toughest kid in his school,
from the poorest family in the poorest street,
he leaves this one a loser, a ghost with a nosebleed
caught between ropes, outclassed and gasping.

All to learn that swagger is not enough,
ability to suffer not enough;
the miles run and the self belief
mean less than the zero in his tally of wins.

For the hard lesson of an easy loss,
the bar-room consolation of admired scars.
At the shop they'll knead his rigid back
before adding *Jesus* to his *Via dolorosa*.

Papyri

*

Somebody's God sent us plagues:
I remember the blood and locusts,
and my father pointing: *Look! Look!*
The lizards were my favourite.

My brother sold his farm,
moved to the new city;
became inspector of drains
for the whole interregnum.

He wrote: *People look sideways*
like thieves expecting to be caught,
or so the village reader claimed,
the month I chose to leave.

*

All the piss and vinegar
of a small town crucifixion.

I was looking at the girls
you get at these things:

pointing at the crossbar,
laughing into their hands.

And their solemn temple faces
when the charge was read.

But he wasn't from round here,
and was still alive when I left.

*

And then I joined the army.
They sent me far to the North.

That winter I wore the skin of a bear
taken from the first man I killed.

It wasn't battle. He was from out of town,
we were drunk on this drink they had.

Nobody seemed to mind.
Traders come and go, but we were army.

Then it was spring, and green,
and the fighting started. We always won.

*

There was one in my company
whose brother knew my brother.
Lived in the same street, he said.

Had I heard of the one true god, he asked.
I said I'd heard of several.
He laughed, and said no, his was different.

His was real, and big with the army.
I should go along one night,
see for myself. No obligation.

There was wine and chanting.
If I ever come home,
I'll tell you my other, secret name.

Hypnogogic

The last bus
to the home you left
swings round the corner
empty. Years ago, now.

The ledger of errors
at one o'clock;
a sleepless dream of gardens
and a broken fence.

Sins of omission. A suit
hanging from the door
strides into the room
with your father's voice.

Psalm 152

For the credulity of children and the white teeth of dogs,
for the job that vanishes in an afternoon,
for the vending machine and the rabbit in the meadow,
for the arguments against your own existence —
Lord, wonderful is thy handiwork.
God of earthquake and aneurism,
of kitten and streptococci,
you surpass yourself, if that is possible,
in the ramifications of leaf and drought.
You are the perfect sunset on the toxic river,
the chocolate box castle on the greenest mountain,
your will is done, whether you like it or not,
and we wait in our cars for your random, infallible judgement.

Security

The train runs empty to the empty town.
Its doors slide open to a platform
where gulls ignore the harsh recorded voice.
There is bird shit, newspapers blown in from elsewhere;
sometimes a paper gusts into a carriage,
and, pinned against a seat, the pages turn
to week-old photographs of motorways
blank as dreams or adverts for new cars.
The doors slide shut, the train will ease away,
gathering speed through the suburbs
and level crossings where no-one waits,
to stop again at the hush of the airport
where, beyond barriers and stalled escalators,
a stray dog will cross the departure lounge,
pause for a moment, ears pricked,
then carry on its frantic, starved routine
caught on official cameras, and unseen.

The Blackpool Illuminations

The manifestos are glossier and contain fewer words. A supplement to a clothing catalogue: natty suits or neat informality. A trend.

The rain is a metaphysical condition. Even when it is not raining, it is raining: an invisible rain that sinks into the bone.

There are pictures of the leader with a cross-section of the electorate. He is smiling.

It rains on the amusement arcades and bingo halls.

Here he is with that beloved ex-statesman. Both of them are smiling. Here he is with his colleagues. They look appropriately serious.

The pier is closed for the winter. Look, it is still raining.

Here is one of him sitting pensively at a desk; here is one of him gazing wide-eyed at what he hopes is the future. Here is one of him talking about his family. There are tears in his eyes: discreet tears, expertly lit.

Discussion documents are left in gentlemen's clubs. They are soaked through; nobody will touch them.

Every word is a euphemism or a prevarication. He recites a slogan and claims it is a policy.

Outside the rain seems to stop. An illusion.

He talks about opportunity and family and hope. The damp souls of delegates steam in the lobbies of business class hotels.

Hope, the final evil in the box.

City planning

Start with the basics:
concrete and wire and water,
the background hum of substations.

Build arcades in the market square,
and let the streets crowd in on every side,
hung with cables, in permanent shade.

Build playgrounds and hairdressers' shops,
narrow cafés where rumours can flourish,
corners where the unemployed will stand.

At night there will be music,
cars driving slowly along the boulevards
where cinemas show the same films every week.

We'll have flagstones for use in barricades,
a slum, our shanty town, and in between
abandoned plots where bodies can be thrown.

In the mornings there will be singing in the schools,
and the old will sit in our parks,
talkative and alone,

as the rivers of their childhood
flow under yellow apartment blocks
and graffiti on the shutters names the missing.

The Apocalypse re-enactment society

We've done the classics:
Thermopylae and Kursk,
a Thirty Years War
that lasted sixty years,
a Leningrad
that will possibly never end.
(I've been there twice. I didn't like the food.)

Afterwards you gather your severed limbs,
you pull the shrapnel from your wounds,
and then it's back to the endless grind
of eternal perfect bliss.
Until, that is, you get that hankering
for the old, human miseries,
and sign up for another massacre.

And every thousand million years or so
we do the big one.
Four beasts, seven angels,
the sea turned to blood —
all this takes work.

It's said Himself disapproves,
but we know he sneaks in to rehearsals —
checking the costumes,
making sure we're keeping to his script.

Every angel wants to be the anti-Christ,
and every one of us will be, eventually.

The neighbours

A *ménàge a trois* by the sound of it
and hours away from terminal dissolution;

caterwauls, ructions, deadfalls and pauses
right through July and murderous August.

I gave up using television to drown it out,
gave up listening to music or bulletins;

gave up thinking out loud, then thinking itself
as I hung on each indistinct word;

until the final, extreme silence,
without one slammed door or thrown switch,

not a lull between storms or a breathless calm:
the absolute dead quiet of nothing at all.

In spite

Our dry mouths
in the afternoon,
the conversation's
monotone.

Your tangled hair,
your arms kept thin
(exercise
and malnutrition).

Led by a face
and tone of voice
I found a grief
and called it love.

Ideal gift

Kept for a best that never came,
it is under a lost scarf
and last year's slippers;

still in the box
after three different cupboards,
three different houses.

The cardboard, powder dry,
keeps a trace of pine and newsprint,
a hint of rain,

while the gift itself
is packed so tight
it barely clinks

and has become a memory,
with no need, now,
to check for cracks

spidering in
from its useless, delicate edge.

Locus desperatus

Memory, like a resentful copyist,
drowsing half the day at the scriptorium;
writing *hammer* for *screwdriver*,
yesterday for *today*, pausing at the lost words.

Or a tableau of Regency daughters:
Aphasia, Agnosia, and pallid Alexia,
their suitor the sharp German doctor
whose name is at the tip of all tongues...

Memory shakes itself awake, and guesses,
writing down whatever fills the space.

Festination. Micrographia

He moves by hoist and leverage,
walks by staggered dips
between chair and table,
keeping to a line across the floor
as if Niagara was underneath.
There are words for this gait,
for his frail, flawed hand on legal forms.
We can calibrate the curve of his spine,
place his skin on a continuum
from elastic to tissue paper,
follow the aetiology of erasure
through every numbered stage
until we reach the zero in the scale.
To hold is to drop. To eat is to choke. To stand is to fall.

Absences

1

No-one mentions the boredom of grief,
how it sits by your shoulder
slowly telling the story of its life

until you know every sigh,
every silence. Grief is dull.
It drinks too much, it doesn't sleep.

You grow sick of listening to its drivel,
sick of knowing, even when it isn't there,
it will be there soon, with its whispers,

its trite condolences,
its burden of tedious guilt:
Forget me, or *Live your own life*.

2

Two days turn into four, four into six,
six days into months, all lost
in a kind of anticipation —

a standing around, as if waiting
for a last bus that may run, or not,
with no way of knowing.

A hard luck story, an apology,
or that familiar ghost at your back;
anything can start it,

this mood that is not your own,
this thought that is not your own.
It is no consolation.

3

The landscape has gaps
that should have been faces or hands.

Blanks and clumsy erasures,
small traces left wherever you look.

The way the grass bends under no-one's feet;
a shadow, cast by no-one, on a wall.

Clothes hang, empty, as a slow breeze
softer than a sleeper's breath, and cold,

comes down off the tundra, the steppes,
moves through the elms and the poplars,

to leave branches unrustled,
no trace of frost on the bent grass.

4

That cinema in the head
where we can screen a final, private cut —

alternative takes,
extended extra scenes,

the backing track we never liked
replaced with schmaltz,

the lines rewritten, redubbed,
given grace and meaning

until everything nearly makes
neat, dramatic sense —

The ending
we still have to live with.

5

Forgetting and not remembering —
what is the difference?

I wake from dreams where nothing is lost
and everything inaccessible

to the news on the radio alarm
that follows, seconds later;

to the slow realisation of absence,
to grief like daylight

filling whatever room I've slept in,
to that tireless voice

keening among the graveyard foliage
of lilies and roses, dark ivy and yew.

The adepts

They have outgrown the shibboleth of coherence
in the afternoon lounge,
abolished the boundaries
between thinking and dreaming.
Some have transcended time
and wait in the lobby for their mothers to collect them
or the Japanese troops to arrive.
In the dining room they insist on their virtues,
the simple intensity of their needs.
Some have gone beyond movement or language:
they stay in their rooms and seem to be watching
though no-one can tell what they see.
We can only guess from their expression
it must be astonishing.